STARS &
PLANETS

▼ The space shuttle *Discovery* leaves the launchpad at the Kennedy Space Center in Florida in April 1990. This mission carried the *Hubble Space Telescope* into orbit around Earth. *Hubble* looks into deep space, revealing distant galaxies as well as the wonders of our own galaxy, the Milky Way.

STARS & PLANETS

Carole Stott

Foreword by
Sir Patrick Moore

SCHOLASTIC INC.

New York Toronto London Auckland Sydney
Mexico City New Delhi Hong Kong Buenos Aires

ISBN-13: 978-0-439-89549-1
ISBN-10: 0-439-89549-9

Copyright © 2005 by Kingfisher Publications Plc. All rights reserved. Published by Scholastic Inc., 557 Broadway, New York, NY 10012, by arrangement with Kingfisher, an imprint of Houghton Mifflin Company. SCHOLASTIC and associated logos are trademarks and/or registered trademarks of Scholastic Inc.

18 17 16 15 14 13   16/0

Printed in the U.S.A.   40

First Scholastic printing, October 2006

Editor: Vicky Weber
Coordinating editor: Caitlin Doyle
Senior designer: Peter Clayman
Picture researcher: Rachael Swann
Senior production controller: Lindsey Scott
DTP manager: Nicky Studdart
DTP operator: Primrose Burton
Artwork archivist: Wendy Allison
Indexer and proofreader: Sheila Clewley

GO FURTHER . . .
INFORMATION PANEL KEY:

 web sites and further reading

 career paths

 places to visit

NOTE TO READERS
The web site addresses listed in this book are correct at the time of publishing. However, due to the ever-changing nature of the Internet, web site addresses and content can change. Web sites can contain links that are unsuitable for children. The publisher cannot be held responsible for changes in web site addresses or content or for information obtained through third-party web sites. We strongly advise that Internet searches are supervised by an adult.

Contents

▼ This view of the rust-colored landscape of Mars was taken by the *Spirit* rover, which landed on the planet in January 2004. *Spirit*'s objective was to study the Martian rocks and soil and search for evidence that liquid water has been on Mars in the past.

Foreword

Astronomy is one of the best of all hobbies. If you make up your mind to take a real interest in it, it can absorb as much—or as little—of your time and energy as you wish. Moreover, it is just about the only science in which amateurs can make useful contributions and in which professional workers are glad to get amateur help. How does a newcomer start out? Obviously by looking up at the sky, reading, and becoming familiar with basic facts. Carole Stott is ideally qualified to provide the right book to excite your interest, and she does just this in *Stars & Planets* in a way that is absorbing and informative.

The book begins by introducing the basic structure of the universe and then goes on to discuss its birth and development, from the big bang, more than 13 billion years ago, up to the present time. It explains how stars are born, how they go through their lives, and how they die—some of them quietly, others violently. We find out how much we can learn from the Sun, to which we owe our very existence and which is the ruler of the solar system—our own particular part of the universe. The focus then turns to our nearest neighbors, the Moon and planets—men have been to the Moon, and space probes have made close studies of all the planets—aside from remote Pluto. All these developments are discussed, and *Stars & Planets* gives the latest information.

Spacecraft also enter the picture, as do the great telescopes that make it possible for us to peer out into the far reaches of the universe and see star systems so remote that their light has taken thousands, millions, or even billions of years to reach us. It is quite amazing how much we have found out in the last few decades. Indeed, things are not quite what we believed them to be only a few years ago—there are no canal-building Martians and no oceans on Venus. However, the excitement is as great as ever, and all of us can share in it.

Reading this book will really broaden your knowledge of the stars and planets. Look at the night sky and find some of the stars and constellations featured in the book, such as Orion, Sirius, and the Great Bear; buy or borrow a pair of binoculars to show you the craters of the Moon, the glorious star fields of the Milky Way, and the rich star clusters such as Orion's Belt. Why not even think about joining your local astronomy club? You will not regret it. Who knows? One day you may discover an exploding star or a brilliant comet!

I wish that I had had this much information when I started out many years ago. Instead let me wish you much pleasure as you read this fascinating and eye-opening book from one of the leading astronomical authors.

Patrick Moore

Sir Patrick Moore has written numerous books on astronomy. Since 1957 he has presented every one of BBC TV's *The Sky at Night* programs, a fact that has earned him a place in the *Guinness Book of Records* as the longest-serving television presenter. In 2001 Sir Patrick received a knighthood from the Queen of Great Britain.

The Sun is the closest star to Earth. Its warmth and light keep us alive, so it is special to us. However, it is just one of billions of stars in the universe.

CHAPTER 1

A universe of stars

Stars surround planet Earth. At night hundreds of them shine as stationary dots of light in a cloudless sky. During the day just one, the brilliant orange-yellow Sun, is on show. It is so close that it outshines all of the other stars in the sky. Many of the stars are like our Sun—they shine brightly and steadily. Others are bigger or smaller, brighter or dimmer, hotter or cooler. Some spin around many times each second, and some explode into space. All of the stars we see belong to our home galaxy—the Milky Way—a huge collection of stars. Billions more galaxies are scattered across the vast distances of space. There are more stars than anything else in the universe—that seemingly endless stretch of space and everything that exists within it.

Vast universe

Whichever way we look out from Earth and however far we peer into space, we see galaxies. There are billions of them—each one is an immense group of stars, gas, and dust. They are scattered throughout space, with huge, virtually empty distances separating neighbors. These galaxies are like remote islands in our vast universe.

Islands in space

Galaxies are huge, and each one consists of billions of stars. Yet galaxies are not the biggest structures in the universe. They are grouped into clusters, which are loosely strung together into superclusters—the biggest structures of all. These are linked across space. Between each supercluster, cluster, and galaxy there are enormous regions of empty space.

◀ Powerful telescopes, such as this one called *Keck*, which is based in Hawaii, let us see deep into the universe.

star

stars exist within galaxies

galaxies exist within clusters

clusters exist within superclusters

▲ The farther we look into space, the more galaxies we see. Here we are gazing deeper than ever before. Our view is part of a photograph taken by the *Hubble Space Telescope* that has revealed almost 10,000 galaxies of different ages, sizes, shapes, and colors. The most distant are around 12 billion light-years away.

Galaxy shapes

The stars in a galaxy stay together because of the pulling force called gravity. Each star follows its own orbit, or path, around the galaxy's center. Together, the stars give a galaxy its shape—there are four basic patterns. Elliptical galaxies are ball-shaped. Spirals are pancake-shaped with a bulging center and two or more arms of stars spiraling outward. Barred spirals have a central bar of stars and arms that wind out from each end. Some galaxies have no particular shape—these are called the irregulars.

Size of the universe

Distances across the universe—or even across a galaxy—are so enormous that the units of measurement used on Earth, such as the mile, are inadequate. Instead measurements across the universe have their own unit called the light-year. One light-year is 5.87 trillion (million million) mi. (9.46 trillion km)—the distance that light travels in one year. That works out to 185,871 mps (299,792km/sec). This is an incredible speed—in fact, light travels quicker than anything else in the universe. The Whirlpool galaxy is around 25 million light-years away. That is much easier than saying that it lies at a distance of 146,600,000,000,000,000,000 mi. (236,500,000,000,000,000,000km)!

▲ The elliptical galaxy M87 is one of the brightest galaxies. It belongs to the Virgo cluster, which consists of more than 2,000 galaxies in a region that is 10 million light-years wide.

▲ The barred spiral galaxy NGC 1300 has an arm of stars spinning away from each end of its central bar. It measures 85,000 light-years from one side to the other.

▲ The Whirlpool galaxy is a spiral galaxy. Young, bright stars make its arms stand out. There are stars in between as well, but they are outshone by the brilliance of the arms.

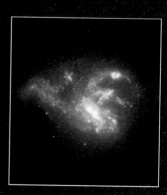

▲ The irregular galaxy NGC 7673 is around 150 million light-years from Earth. Like other irregulars, it is rich in gas and dust and is always busy producing new stars.

Bang!

The universe has existed for more than 13 billion years. Astronomers have worked out that it all started in an explosion called the big bang. This was the start of everything—the start of time, space, and all that there is in the universe. Back then the universe looked nothing like it does now. It was unbelievably small, unbearably hot, and consisted of tiny fragments of energy. From the instant of creation the universe has been changing into the one we know today.

8.3 light-minutes from Earth

▲ We see the Sun as it was eight minutes and 19 seconds ago. It is 8.3 light-minutes from Earth—92.8 million mi. (149.6 million km).

Looking back in time

Amazingly, we can look back in time and see the universe long ago. We can do this thanks to light—the fastest traveler in the universe. Turn on a lamp, and its light seems to reach your eyes instantly. Turn it off, and the light is gone. If the Sun was turned off, it would be more than eight minutes before we would notice. That is how long it takes for sunlight to reach Earth. The light from distant stars and galaxies takes much longer to reach us. When we look at them, we see them as they were when light left them billions of years ago. Some of the most distant galaxies ever found are around 12 billion light-years away. This means that it has taken around 12 billion years for their light to reach us, so we see these galaxies as they were when the universe was very young.

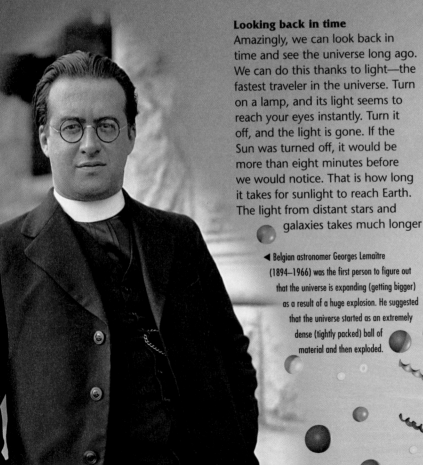

◀ Belgian astronomer Georges Lemaître (1894–1966) was the first person to figure out that the universe is expanding (getting bigger) as a result of a huge explosion. He suggested that the universe started as an extremely dense (tightly packed) ball of material and then exploded.

8.6 light-years from Earth

▲ The brightest star in Earth's night sky is Sirius (center top) in the constellation Canis Major. Its light takes 8.6 years to reach us.

2.4 million light-years from Earth

▲ The spiral-shaped Andromeda galaxy measures roughly around 150,000 light-years from side to side (.87 quintillion mi. or 1.4 quintillion km).

11 billion light-years from Earth

▲ We are looking at these galaxies just two billion years after the big bang, at a time when many giant galaxies were forming.

Back to the beginning

At the very beginning the universe was super hot and ultra dense; it has been cooling and getting bigger ever since. Even before the first trillionth of a second was over, the universe had ballooned in size. In less than one second it had cooled to 18 billion °F (10 billion °C), and its energy particles became tiny pieces of matter—the building blocks of all the material in today's universe. At the end of three minutes the first elements—hydrogen and helium—had formed. By then around three fourths of the universe was hydrogen, and almost all the rest was helium. The universe stayed similar to this for the next 250,000 years, although it continued to cool and grow bigger. All this time the universe was opaque, which means that it was sort of foggy, and light could not pass through it. So when we look back at far distant stars and galaxies, we can only go back to around 300,000 years after the big bang—telescopes cannot show us what it was like before that time.

▼ The time line below continues on pages 12 and 13. It shows the evolution of the universe from the big bang right up to today. The scale below the blue line shows how much time has passed since the big bang happened. The captions above the blue line tell you what is happening in the universe within each gray band.

The universe began in an explosion around 13 billion years ago.

The universe was made up of energy that turned into tiny particles of matter within seconds. At this time it was opaque—you could not see through it.

It grew bigger and cooled but remained opaque.

| 0 | 1 trillionth of a second | 1 minute | 1 year | 1,000 years | 300,000 years |

Changing universe

The universe has been changing throughout its entire lifetime. Every aspect of it, such as its size, temperature, and structure, has evolved. Only the amount of material in the universe has remained constant. But even this matter has changed in substance. The original elements, hydrogen and helium, have in turn produced all the other elements that now exist. Changes have been on a large scale and taken billions of years, and they continue today.

The universe was now cool enough to make atoms, and it became transparent.

The atoms started to clump together in cloudy wisps.

Over millions of years clouds formed.

The clouds gradually turned into stars.

By the time the universe was a few billion years old it consisted of galaxies of stars.

| 300,000 years | 300 million years | 1 billion years | 3 billion years |

The first stars and galaxies

By around 300,000 years after the big bang, the universe had cooled to roughly 5,432°F (3,000°C). Atoms of hydrogen and helium formed, and the universe became transparent (see-through), as it is today. Very slowly over the next few million years the material started to gather and form denser regions. These grew in size over millions more years and developed into thick clouds as more and more material clumped together. Eventually the clouds formed into balls and became stars. Collections of these stars were the first galaxies.

The changing face of the universe

Over the next few billion years the rest of the galaxies in the universe formed. Today's galaxies look different from the original ones because there is constant change in the universe. Galaxies collide and reshape, stars evolve and die, and new stars are born.

Bigger and bigger

The universe is getting larger all the time. We know this because the galaxies are still rushing away after the big bang explosion. As the universe expands, it becomes cooler and less concentrated.

The missing universe

When we look into space, we detect billions of galaxies and stars scattered through billions of light-years. Yet scientists are sure that all we see and know about the universe is only a fraction of what is there. As much as 95 percent of the universe is still to be discovered. This missing part is called "dark matter." It was produced along with the other material in the big bang—the type that is in galaxies and stars. Dark matter is different; it is thought to be tiny particles of energy, much smaller than atoms. But astronomers will only know for certain when the dark matter is found.

▶ Changes on Earth are all part of the continuing change in the universe. Wind, rain, volcanoes, and humans all play their part in altering Earth's surface. By building towns and cities, such as New York City (shown here), people make an enormous difference to the planet.

Galaxies are huge, but they only take up a tiny fraction—less than two millionths—of space.

today

Home galaxy

It is impossible to know exactly how many galaxies exist. Astronomers estimate that there are around 100–125 billion. There is one galaxy that we know much better than the others. In astronomical terms it does not stand out from the crowd, but to us it is special. It is the Milky Way, our home galaxy. It consists of at least 500 billion stars, one of which is our Sun.

◄ The American astronomer Edwin Hubble (1889–1953) was the first person to show that there are galaxies beyond our own and that they are constantly moving away from the Milky Way.

Inside the Milky Way

Astronomers believe that the Milky Way is a barred spiral galaxy. It is difficult to be sure because we are inside it. All we can see is a mixture of full spiral arms and short segments coming out of a central bulge, but not the Milky Way's complete shape. It is like being inside a forest and trying to figure out its size and shape and how many trees it is made up of. The Sun is around 25,000 light-years from

▼ This is what astronomers think that the Milky Way looks like from the outside. It is disk shaped, measuring around 100,000 light-years across and around 4,000 light-years from top to bottom. The central bulge gets its color from the many red and yellow old stars that it contains. Hotter, younger stars color the disk blue-white.

▶ Before technology allowed us to understand stars and galaxies as we do today, people used myths and stories to explain what they could see in the sky. In this painting by Tintoretto (1518–1594), the goddess Juno is feeding baby Hercules. According to Roman myth, drops of spilled milk formed the Milky Way.

Local Group

The Milky Way is part of a cluster of around 30 galaxies called the Local Group galaxy cluster. Most of them are small—the biggest are the Milky Way and the Andromeda galaxy, which is one of the biggest spirals known. It is 2.4 million light-years away and is the most distant object that we can see by using only our eyes.

the center of the Milky Way. From our inside position we get good views of many of the galaxy's individual objects. Around 90 percent of what we can see is stars, and the rest is gas and dust. The dust limits our view of the center. This is a very active and crowded place and is home to an immense black hole (see page 22) that is millions of times more massive than the Sun. The stars in the Milky Way orbit (travel around) the center, all going in the same direction. The Sun completes an orbit every 220 million years.

▲ From our position inside the Milky Way we can look through it. We see so many stars that their light merges and makes a milky band across our dark sky. The band is broadest and brightest as we look toward the center of the galaxy (in the middle of this image).

Star material

Temperature scale
72,000°F (40,000°C)
45,000°F (25,000°C)
18,000°F (10,000°C)
12,600°F (7,000°C)
9,900°F (5,500°C)
8,100°F (4,500°C)
3,600°F (2,000°C)

Stars are gigantic, spinning balls of hot, glowing gas that shine throughout the universe. The one closest to Earth—the Sun—appears to be huge to us and seems to outshine the rest. At night we can see many other stars in the sky—small pinpoints of light set against the darkness of space. Their huge distance from Earth makes them seem tiny and dim. In fact some are bigger and brighter than the Sun, while others are smaller and duller. They all have individual characteristics and differ in size, temperature, brightness, color, and mass.

▲ The Sun is by far the brightest star seen from Earth. Its light floods the sky. Other stars become visible only when the Sun is below the horizon and the sky is dark. The Sun is orange-yellow in color—this means that it has a temperature of around 9,900°F (5,500°C).

▲ The hottest stars are blue, the coolest are red. Stars in the night sky all look like pinpoints of white light because they are so faraway. To see a star's true color, astronomers closely examine the light.

Temperature and color

All stars are incredibly hot, but some are even hotter than others. The hottest are around 72,000°F (40,000°C), and the coolest are 3,600°F (2,000°C). The color of a star depends on its surface temperature (see chart above). There are seven main types of stars based on color and temperature.

Shape, size, and mass

All stars are ball-shaped. No stars are star-shaped, and they do not twinkle—they just look like it when their light passes through Earth's atmosphere.

Stars are made up of hydrogen gas with some helium, which is pulled into a ball shape by the star's gravity. There is a different quantity of gas in each star. This amount is called the star's mass, and it does not change once a star has formed.

Mass is not the same as size: a star with more mass than the Sun is made up of more material; a star with a greater size is wider. A big star does not have to be a massive star—it can just mean that its gas is spread out. Some massive stars are very small because their gas is densely packed.

▼ Stars come in a range of sizes. In relation to the Sun, a dwarf star is approximately 100 times smaller; a giant star is typically 30 to 50 times bigger; a blue supergiant is around 100 times bigger; and a red supergiant is up to a few hundred times bigger. The stars below are not shown in their actual position in the sky.

dwarf star (around 14,400°F, or 8,000°C)

Sun (around 9,900°F, or 5,500°C)

blue supergiant (more than 18,000°F, or 10,000°C)

▲ The Sun is not as bright when it is seen from Pluto, as in the view above. It looks much dimmer, like a faint point of light, when it is seen from even farther away. The reason that it looks big to us is that it is very close to Earth.

► Stars shine because of activity in their core, or center. Deep inside the Sun hydrogen is being converted to helium, and energy is produced. Much of this energy leaves the Sun as light and heat.

outer layer

inner layer

core

surface
(photosphere)

Brightness

A star has two types of brightness. The first, called "absolute magnitude," is a measure of the real brightness of a star. It compares the stars as if they were all the same distance from us. The second measure, called "apparent magnitude," is the brightness that we can see from Earth, and it compares the stars at their actual, varied distances from us. The Sun is the brightest star on the apparent magnitude scale. But if you lined it up with the other stars all at the same distance, it would look dim.

► The two brightest stars in Orion are Betelgeuse (top left) and Rigel (bottom right). Betelgeuse is a red supergiant with a surface temperature of around 5,400°F (3,000°C). Rigel's surface temperature is roughly 21,600°F (12,000°C), which means that it is a blue-white star.

giant star
(around 8,100°F, or
4,500°C)

red supergiant
(less than 8,100°F,
or 4,500°C)

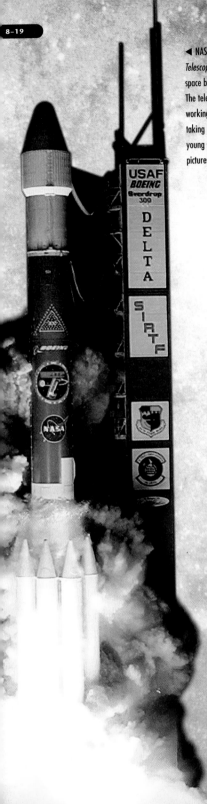

◀ NASA's *Spitzer Space Telescope* was launched into space by this *Delta* rocket. The telescope has been working in space since 2003, taking photographs of very young stars. (See one of its pictures on page 19, bottom.)

A star is born

Stars are created in enormous clouds of gas and dust inside galaxies. Over hundreds of thousands of years this gas and dust come together and make hundreds or thousands of mini-clouds. Each of these then develops into a spinning ball of gas called a protostar—this is the first sign of a new star. In its center is densely packed gas, which will produce the energy to turn the protostar into a dazzling fully fledged star.

Turning on a star

Gravity pulls the gas in a protostar toward its center. As the gas gets more squashed, it gets hotter and hotter. The densest, hottest gas is in the core. When this reaches roughly 18 billion °F (10 billion °C), a nuclear reaction starts.

The hydrogen in the core turns into helium, and energy is produced. Two forms of this energy are light and heat. The star has now switched on and will shine steadily for many millions or billions of years.

◀ In the past before scientists had any alternative theories about star birth, people made up stories to explain how the stars were born. According to Greek mythology for example, the maiden Callisto, seen here riding a chariot, was turned into a bear by the goddess Artemis. A whirlwind carried her up to the sky, where she became the Great Bear constellation.

Star clusters

Stars are made together in groups called star clusters. A group of young, newly "turned on" stars is called an open cluster. Often the stars in the cluster drift apart over millions of years. However, some groups stay together—these are known as globular clusters. The Sun was born in a cluster, probably with a twin star, but the twins and the other stars have drifted apart and now exist alone.

Life span

The length of a star's life is dictated by its mass—the amount of material that it is made of. The Sun, and stars of a similar mass, live for around 10 billion years. The Sun is around halfway through its life span. Stars with a greater mass have shorter lives. The most massive last only a few million years. Stars with a lower mass have the longest life spans—they live for many billions of years.

◀ Bright, young stars light up the enormous rosebud-shaped cloud of gas and dust that has produced them. There are around 130 young stars in this cloud, known as NGC 7129.

◀ Massive stars are forming inside a cloud of gas and dust nicknamed the Papillon. This is in the Large Magellanic Cloud galaxy, around 170,000 light-years from Earth.

The story of a star

Stars shine steadily for most of their lives. During this time they are called main-sequence stars—the Sun is one of these. As stars get older they change and eventually die. Some stars take millions of years to die, and in the process they turn into some of the most beautiful and brightly colored stars that we can see in our galaxy. Other stars cut their lives short when they blast themselves across space in one gigantic explosion.

▼ Stars made all the elements in the universe such as oxygen and carbon. This means that the elements, which make up all that there is on Earth—including human beings—were star material long ago.

From giant to dwarf

The pattern and length of a star's life and death depend on its mass—the amount of material it is made up of. Stars like the Sun, and those made up of up to around eight times the Sun's mass, all die slowly. This process starts when the star runs out of hydrogen gas that it needs to convert into heat and light. It swells, cools, and becomes a red giant. Eventually it pushes away its outer layers of gas, which form a bright and colorful envelope around the dying star. At this colorful stage the star is called a planetary nebula, and it stays like this for tens of thousands of years until the gas disperses into space. Then all that is left are the remains of the original star, called a white dwarf. This cools, shrinks, and dies over billions of years.

▼ This planetary nebula is nicknamed the Ant because of the shape of its gas. Deep within this at the center is the dying star. It will take tens of thousands of years for the gas to spread out into space, and by this time the star will have shrunk, dimmed, and cooled.

◄ ▲ A young, blue star made up of around 20 times the mass of the Sun exploded in the nearby galaxy, the Large Magellanic Cloud, in February 1987. The two photographs above show the star before it exploded (left) and the supernova just a few weeks after the explosion (right). Both pictures cover the same area of sky.

Stellar explosion

Stars that are made up of more than eight times the Sun's mass can blow themselves apart in a gargantuan explosion. The star begins life as one of the crowd, but suddenly it explodes and becomes an outstandingly bright and eye-catching new, super star, called a supernova. This can take several months to fade from view. The huge amount of gas and dust that it blasts into space is called a supernova remnant. The core of the original star is left behind after the explosion. Depending on the mass of this core, the star then becomes either a black hole or a neutron star (see pages 22–23).

Recycling

Material discarded by old stars and blasted off by exploding stars slowly disperses into space. Eventually it joins with other gas and dust to form enormous clouds, from which new stars take shape over billions of years (see page 18).

Black holes & neutron stars

Some space objects are not like the usual stars and galaxies—they are much more extreme. For example, a neutron star is only around the size of a city, but it is made up of more material than the Sun. It is the smallest and densest type of star that we can see. At the other end of the scale are galactic black holes. These were made in the young universe, and they have been devouring anything that comes too close ever since.

Galactic black holes

Some galaxies have large amounts of energy—much more than comes from their stars alone. This power comes from the center of the galaxy. It is produced by stellar material falling into a galactic black hole, which was formed when the galaxy was born. At that early stage gravity pulled at the stars and gas at the galaxy's center. They became so squashed that they collapsed inward to form an incredibly dense galactic black hole. These have such intense gravity that nothing can ever escape, not even light, which is the reason why the hole is black.

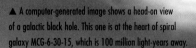

▲ A computer-generated image shows a head-on view of a galactic black hole. This one is at the heart of spiral galaxy MCG-6-30-15, which is 100 million light-years away.

◀ A black hole rips a star apart. The overpowering gravity of the black hole pulls at the star's material. It forms a disk of swirling gas before everything disappears into the hole forever.

Stellar black holes

Smaller, stellar black holes can form from supernova explosions if the star's core is more than three times the Sun's mass. The core's material is crushed by gravity and collapses inward. The star gets smaller and denser as it collapses more and more. Eventually the star is so small and dense that it becomes a hole in space.

▲ A neutron star discovered by its pulses is known as a pulsar. It beams energy into space. The star's magnetic field (turquoise in this computer-generated image) channels the energy into two beams, one on each side of the star.

▶ The American scientist Robert Oppenheimer (1904–1967) helped us understand neutron stars and black holes. He figured out that neutron stars are always less than around three times the Sun's mass.

Neutrons

Supernova cores that are less than three times the Sun's mass collapse inward to produce neutron stars. These are unlike any other stars— they are very small by comparison and have a tough, solid surface. They are also extremely dense— a piece the size of a cherry would weigh more than 100 million tons on Earth. Like all other stars they spin, but these stars do it extremely quickly—up to several hundred times per second.

Pulsars

Some neutron stars are called pulsars. The star is the same, but a stream of energy is channeled away from it in two beams. As the star spins, its beams sweep around, sending pulses of energy into space. This is similar to the way that a lighthouse sends shafts of light across the sea at night.

The closest star

There is one star that we can see
in detail—the Sun. All other stars are
light-years away, while the Sun is just over
eight light-minutes away from Earth. We
can see features on its raging surface—its
planet-sized dark spots and its jets and
flares of gas shooting into space. The
Sun has a family of rock and gas objects,
including Earth, that orbits around it. We
humans think of the Sun and its family as
special. But other stars have planets, too.

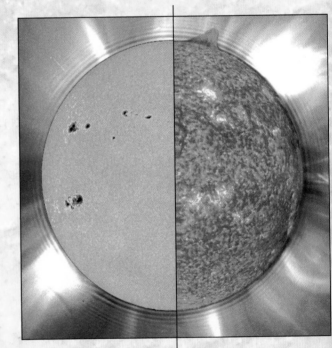

▲ Dark sunspots stand out on the Sun's face.
They are cooler areas that appear where hot
gas cannot reach the surface. They usually
last for weeks at a time.

▲ Large flares and loops of hot gas explode
often over the sunspots (shown on the picture
above as white patches). Huge sheets of hot
gas extend out from the Sun.

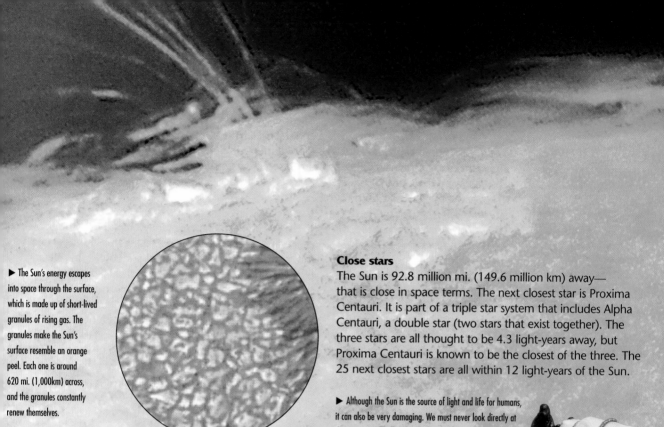

▶ The Sun's energy escapes into space through the surface, which is made up of short-lived granules of rising gas. The granules make the Sun's surface resemble an orange peel. Each one is around 620 mi. (1,000km) across, and the granules constantly renew themselves.

The Sun

The Sun is not solid—it is made up of gases. These are mostly hydrogen and helium with tiny amounts of around 90 other elements. Like everything in the universe, it spins. Unlike Earth, which is rigid and spins as a whole, the parts of the Sun take different amounts of time to spin. The equator takes 25 days, and the polar regions take more than 30 days to rotate once.

The diameter (width) of the Sun is approximately .89 million mi. (1.4 million km)—around 109 times that of Earth. The photosphere—its visible surface—is 9,900°F (5,500°C), and its core is 27 million °F (15 million °C). Above its surface is its gas atmosphere, which stretches for millions of miles into space.

Stars with planets

When a star is formed, it does not use up all the material in its original cloud of gas and dust. A lot is pushed off into space, and some can produce planets. The cloud surrounding the star spins and slowly flattens into a disk. This disk material gradually joins to form planets, which all orbit the star at the center. We know of more than 135 planets orbiting stars outside our solar system.

Close stars

The Sun is 92.8 million mi. (149.6 million km) away—that is close in space terms. The next closest star is Proxima Centauri. It is part of a triple star system that includes Alpha Centauri, a double star (two stars that exist together). The three stars are all thought to be 4.3 light-years away, but Proxima Centauri is known to be the closest of the three. The 25 next closest stars are all within 12 light-years of the Sun.

▶ Although the Sun is the source of light and life for humans, it can also be very damaging. We must never look directly at the Sun—even during a solar eclipse—as the brightness could blind us. We must also be careful when we go out in the Sun—always wear sunblock and cover up well.

▼ The Sun provides all the energy for life on Earth. Not surprisingly many cultures, such as the Mayans, who lived in South America around 2,000 years ago, have worshipped the Sun as a god.

SUMMARY OF CHAPTER 1: A UNIVERSE OF STARS

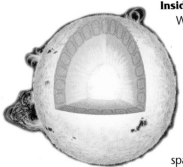

The Sun, with
a cutaway section
showing the core
and inner layers

Inside the universe

We have taken our first look into the universe and found out what it is made up of on a large scale. We have seen that it is full of galaxies and that these exist in every part of the universe: in nearby space, in the distant reaches of space, and everywhere in between. Each one of the galaxies is brimming with countless stars. We have also discovered that the universe is huge, and it is getting bigger all the time.

Going back to the beginning

For around 70 years astronomers have known that the universe is full of galaxies and that it is expanding. These discoveries have made astronomers realize that the universe was smaller in the past and that the galaxies were once closer together. Over the years astronomers have pieced together everything they have found out about the stars and galaxies. They now know that the first of these was formed more than 12 billion years ago in the young universe, and that the universe started around 13 billion years ago with an explosion that they call the big bang.

The stellar cycle

The universe has been constantly changing throughout its lifetime. Not only on a large scale but in other ways too. Stars exist for only a limited period of time. Like humans, they are born, they change and develop during their lives, and then they die. The gas and dust that they are made from is recycled—the material pushed away by a dying star eventually becomes part of a new star. The Sun, the closest star to us, is no exception—it is also changing. Deep inside it is converting hydrogen into helium. This does not make any difference to the way that it looks now, but in around 5 billion years' time the Sun will have grown bigger and changed color. At that stage, it will be a red giant star.

Go further . . .

Look deep into the universe with the *Hubble Space Telescope* at: www.hubblesite.org

To find out more about the galaxies and stars, including our Sun, go to: www.jpl.nasa.gov/stars_galaxies

Test your knowledge of the universe or have fun building a galaxy at: www.hubblesite.org/fun_.and._games

If your questions about the universe are still unanswered, ask an astronomer at: http://coolcosmos. ipac.caltech.edu/cosmic_kids/AskKids

To the Ends of the Universe by Heather Couper and Nigel Henbest (Dorling Kindersley, 1998)

Astronomer
Studies the universe and everything that is in it.

Astrophysicist
An astronomer who examines the physics of objects in the universe.

Cosmologist
Looks at the origin, evolution, and future of the universe.

Galactic astronomer
Studies the origin, evolution, and makeup of galaxies.

Solar astronomer
Examines the closest star, the Sun.

Stellar astronomer
Investigates the stars.

Visit one of the best observatories in the U.S.A.—the home of the Discovery Channel Telescope and also where Pluto was discovered! Lowell Observatory 1400 W. Mars Hill Road Flagstaff, AZ 86001 Phone: (928) 774-3358 www.lowell.edu

Visit the first planetarium built in the Western hemisphere, and check out the fun exhibition area: The Adler Planetarium and Astronomy Museum 1300 S. Lake Shore Drive Chicago, IL 60605 Phone: (312) 922-7827 www.adlerplanetarium.org

CHAPTER 2

The Sun & its family

A small, bluish ball of rock is our space home. It is the planet called Earth, and it belongs to the solar system. This is our local space neighborhood, containing the Sun and its family of planets, moons, space rocks, and comets. This part of space seems enormous to us, but really the solar system is just a tiny part of one galaxy, the Milky Way, which is in among millions of galaxies

The Sun is the largest, most important central member of our neighborhood, and all the other objects that make up the solar system follow paths around it. Next in size after the Sun come the planets. Some of these are rocky, others are made mostly of gas, several are bigger, others are small. But none is covered in water like Earth, nor has life

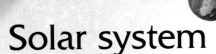

Solar system

The Sun and its family are known as the solar system. The Sun—the only star in the system—is the largest family member, making up around 99 percent of the solar system's mass. There are eight planets, more than 140 moons, and trillions of space rocks and comets. They were all made around 4.6 billion years ago from a cloud of gas and dust and have been together ever since.

◄ The astronomer William Herschel (1738–1822) discovered the planet Uranus in 1781. Six planets have been known of since ancient times (Mercury, Venus, Earth, Mars, Jupiter, and Saturn). Neptune was discovered in 1846 and Pluto in 1930.

▲ Eight planets orbit the Sun. Closest in are the four rock planets: Mercury, Venus, Earth, and Mars. Just two of them, Earth and Mars, have moons.

Family members

The planets form two main groups. The four closest to the Sun—Mercury, Venus, Earth, and Mars—are rocky and are known as the rock, or inner, planets. Of these only Earth and Mars have moons. Then come Jupiter, Saturn, Uranus, and Neptune—the gas giants, or outer planets. These huge planets are mostly made up of gas, with small, solid, rocky centers. They all have moons, and rings of icy rock pieces encircle them.

A ring of space rocks called the Main Belt, which is between Mars and Jupiter, separates the two groups. Beyond Neptune is Pluto, which is a dwarf planet and an object in the Edgeworth-Kuiper Belt, and the Oort Cloud, which is made up of comets.

5
Jupiter

◀ Jupiter is the largest object in the solar system after the Sun. It is one of the four gas giants. The others, in order of size and distance from the Sun, are Saturn, Uranus, and Neptune. All four are encircled by rings and have families of moons. The most distant and smallest planet of all is Pluto.

6
Saturn

Origins

The solar system was produced from the Solar Nebula, a vast, spinning cloud of gas and dust. The Sun was formed first, then its family. Tiny pieces of material joined to make larger and larger objects. Material close to the Sun produced the rocky planets—Mercury, Venus, Earth, and Mars. The more distant outer planets—Jupiter, Saturn, Uranus, and Neptune—were rocky balls at the start. They captured gas, which made enormous atmospheres around their solid cores, and so formed today's gas giants.

Shape of the solar system

The Sun is in the center of the solar system. Its gravity holds all the other family members in orbit. Each object follows its own path around the Sun, and as it travels, it spins. The path is its orbit, and a completed circuit is known as one orbit.

The planets all travel around the Sun in the same direction and on a similar plane (flat surface). This means that the planetary part of the solar system is flat and almost circular. It stretches out around 3 billion mi. (6 billion km) from the Sun.

Comets orbit in any plane, so some comets go above and some go below the Sun. They form a 9-trillion-mi. (15-trillion-km)-wide ball around the planetary part of the solar system.

7
Uranus

8
Neptune

▲ All the planets orbit the Sun, and they all travel in the same direction, spinning as they go.

▶ The bright dot in the middle of this image is the planetary part of the solar system. Surrounding this is the vast ball-shaped cloud of comets, the Oort Cloud.

Home planet

An extraordinary ball of rock, 7,909 mi. (12,756km) in diameter, lies 92.8 million mi. (149.6 million km) from the Sun. It speeds around it every 365.25 days, racing along at almost 19 mps (30km/sec). This ball is the largest of all the rock planets. It has oxygen in its atmosphere and water on its surface. It is a dynamic world that is full of life. Welcome to planet Earth—our home—with its lifeless companion—one fourth of its size—the Moon.

Earth

Our home planet has many unique features. It is the only one we know of that has life. The oxygen-rich atmosphere—its second unique feature—supports that life. Living on Earth is comfortable—the average temperature is 59°F (15°C), so its third characteristic is that the water can be liquid. In fact, Earth is the only planet with liquid water on its surface. Its fourth unique feature is the crust—the shell of rock covering Earth. It is the only planetary crust that is split into plates, or moving parts, which collide or move apart and renew the surface.

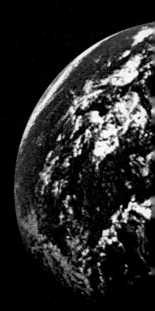

◄ The Moon is easily seen in Earth's sky. It is larger and brighter than any other nighttime object. When the side facing us is completely lit up by the Sun, it is a full moon.

▼▶ The Earth looks large in the Moon's sky. When seen from the Moon, our home planet appears to be blue because 71 percent of the surface is covered in water. Unlike Earth, the Moon's surface has changed little in the past 1.6 billion years or so. The dark areas are the Moon's maria; the lighter areas are older highlands covered in craters.

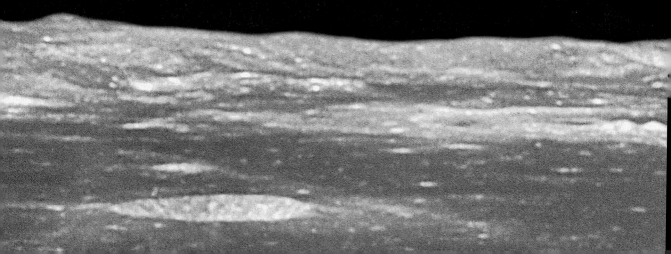

The Moon

This dry ball of rock was formed around 4.5 billion years ago. A planet-sized rock crashed into young Earth and splashed material from Earth into space. Slowly the material came together into a ball, the Moon.

The young Moon was bombarded by space rocks. As the rocks hit the surface, they formed bowl-shaped hollows, called impact craters—many of which can still be seen today. Around three billion years ago lava from volcanoes that were active at the time flooded some of the craters and formed the Moon's enormous plains, called maria.

Earth–Moon partnership

The Moon travels with Earth around the Sun. The Moon orbits Earth, and both spin as they go. Earth spins once every 23.9 hours, the Moon spins every 27.3 days. It also takes 27.3 days for the Moon to orbit Earth, so the same side—the nearside—always faces us.

The Sun lights both Earth and the Moon—on each, one side has sunlight when it is nighttime on the other side. That is why on Earth daytime in Australia is nighttime in Europe.

▲ Many factors shape Earth's landscape—the range of temperatures, types of land, the atmosphere, and living things. All in all we live on a varied and rich planet.

The shape of the Moon

As the Moon moves around Earth, we see changing phases of it in our sky. To us, the Moon's shape seems to vary between the complete circle of a full moon and the almost invisible new moon. What we actually see is the part of the nearside that is lit by the Sun at that time.

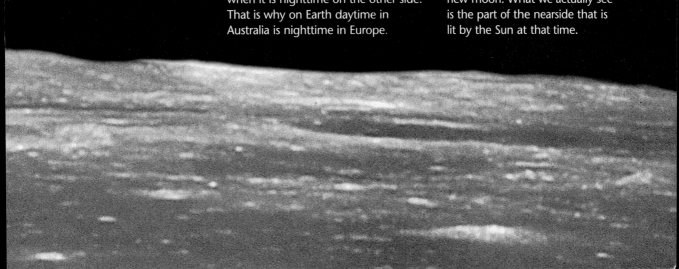

The rock planets

Mercury, Venus, and Mars lie close to Earth, and they, like our home planet, are balls of rock. The four were made of the same material over the same period of time, but today they are very different worlds. Mercury is a dry, barren planet. Venus is shrouded by a thick blanket of poisonous gas. Frozen, rock-strewn deserts cover cold Mars.

Atmospheres
Anyone looking at Earth from space can easily see its surface. This is because its atmosphere, the layer of gas covering it, is mostly transparent. Mars has a much thinner atmosphere, and Mercury's is almost nonexistent. So we also have a clear view of these planets. Venus is different—a thick atmosphere surrounds it. This stops us from seeing Venus' surface, and it also traps in heat from the Sun. This means that Venus has an average temperature of 867°F (464°C)— it is the hottest planet of all.

▲ The planet Mercury is named after Mercury, the messenger to the Roman gods. The messenger always has wings on his cap.

▼ Mercury's surface is covered with impact craters. It also has cracks, ridges, and wrinkles, which were formed when the young hot planet cooled, shrank, and its spin slowed down.

Volcanic change
The surfaces of all four rock planets have been changed by volcanoes. With Mercury this was in the distant past, and there are no active volcanoes left today. But on Venus, Earth, and Mars changes continued. Venus could be volcanically active again, and we know that our planet is—around 50 volcanoes erupt on Earth each year. The volcanoes on Mars are not expected to erupt again soon, but they could in the future.

Cratered world
Space rocks bombarded the rock planets when they were young, around 4 billion years ago. As a rock hit a planet, it formed an impact crater. Most of the craters on Venus, Earth, and Mars were destroyed as the surfaces of these planets renewed themselves, for example by volcanic activity. Mercury still bears the scars of the rock attack, as the planet has remained almost unaltered over the years. The only visible changes on Mercury are plains that formed in the distant past when lava from then live volcanoes flowed across its surface.

▲ Mars, like Earth, has white polar caps of ice. The north polar region (1) is easily seen in this view of Mars by the *Hubble Space Telescope*. Farther south is the Valles Marineris (2), which cuts across the planet. It is a vast canyon system, 2,790 mi. (4,500km) long and 5 mi. (8km) deep.

▼ Venus has more than 1,600 major volcanoes. Maat Mons is one of the largest—it is 6 mi. (9km) high with a base that is 124 mi. (200km) across. Solid lava extends for many hundreds of miles into the surrounding area.

Space rocks

Countless space rocks travel around the Sun. Most of them are in the Main Belt, which is an enormous doughnut-shaped racetrack of rocks between Mars and Jupiter. A second, flat belt of icy rock objects, the Edgeworth-Kuiper Belt, lies beyond Neptune. The material in both these belts, plus billions of other chunks that circle the four giant planets, is leftover material from the time when the planets were formed.

The Main Belt
Billions of space rocks called asteroids make up the Main Belt, also known as the Asteroid Belt. Each cold, dead, rocky, metallic asteroid takes around three to six years to orbit the Sun, spinning every nine hours or so as it goes. At 578 mi. (933km) across, circular Ceres is the largest asteroid. Only those larger than around 198 mi. (320km) are round; most are irregular potato shapes. Around one billion or so are between .6 mi. (1km) and 155 mi. (250km) across, and there are more that are even smaller. Yet the belt is not crowded—thousands of miles separate an asteroid from its neighbor.

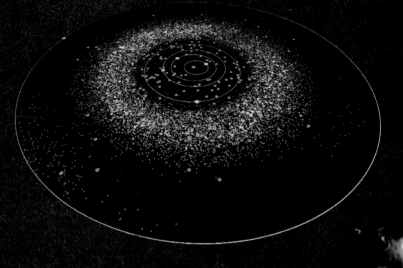

▲ More than 90 percent of all asteroids (here as green dots) are in the Main Belt between the orbits of Mars and Jupiter. Some other asteroids (red dots) follow paths that take them within Earth's orbit. A group of asteroids called the Trojans (small blue dots) travel around the Sun close to Jupiter's orbit.

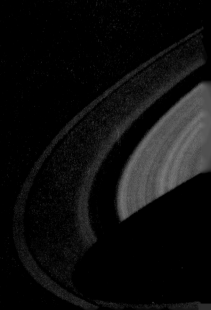

▲ Eros is 20 mi. (33km) long. It started life in the Main Belt of asteroids but now follows a path that crosses Earth's orbit.

Planetary rings
The four largest planets—Jupiter, Saturn, Uranus, and Neptune—are all encircled by rings. None of the rings are solid bands. Each is a collection of grains, chunks, and boulders, which are made up of material that ranges from ice to rock. Saturn's rings contain the most material—at least one million times that of Jupiter's. Its icy pieces reflect the light well and make the rings easy to see.

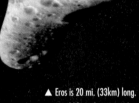

▲ Gaspra is an asteroid. It 12 mi. (19km) long and orbit the Sun every 3.3 years at the inner edge of the Main Belt.

▶ Saturn's rings look solid but are made up of pieces of icy rock, which range in size from around 16 ft. (5m) across. The rings look green in the picture because of the way that the photograph was taken. Turn to page 48 to see the ring in their light.

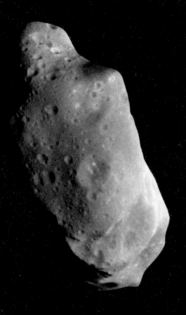

The Edgeworth-Kuiper Belt

This belt consists of icy space rocks that are more like the snowy nucleus of a comet (see page 41) than a rocky asteroid.

The belt stretches from near the orbit of Neptune to far beyond Pluto and merges with the Oort Cloud—the realm of the comets (see page 40). The belt is believed to be home to around 60,000 cometlike objects larger than 31 mi. (50km) across. More than 700 have been found so far.

Astronomers determined that Pluto is part of this group— it is an icy rock and unlike any of its large planetary neighbors.

▲ ▶ The craters on the surface of the 36-mi. (58-km)-long asteroid Ida were formed by smaller asteroids smashing into it. Ida's small moon, 1-mi. (1.5-km)-wide Dactyl, orbits it (right).

▶ Clyde Tombaugh (1906–1997) was an American astronomer. He could not afford to go to college, so he built his own telescope to study the stars and planets. He became an assistant at Lowell Observatory in Flagstaff, Arizona. Night after night he searched the sky for a ninth planet. In 1930 he found a tiny object outside Neptune's orbit, which was named Pluto.

Jupiter was the king of the Roman gods and the ruler of the heavens. He was believed to control storms and is often shown hurling a thunderbolt, as in this Italian painting from the 1500s and this marble statue. Named after the god, the stormy planet Jupiter is the "king" of the planets because of its enormous size.

Planetary giants

Four of the planets—Jupiter, Saturn, Uranus, and Neptune—have a lot in common: they are giants compared to the other planets, and they are all gaseous. They are mostly made up of hydrogen and helium, with small amounts of other chemical elements. None of them have solid surfaces, and when we look at them, we see their colorful gas atmospheres, but deep below the surface are small, round centers of rock. As a result of their size and makeup, these four planetary giants are often described as the gas giants.

Uranus and Neptune

The methane gas in Uranus and Neptune gives these two planets their blue-green coloring. Uranus stands out from all the other planets because it lies on its side. It is thought that young Uranus was knocked into this position by a giant space rock in the distant past. Its neighbor, Neptune, has bizarre weather. Energy from the Sun heats up Earth and drives its weather, but cold Neptune is 30 times farther away from the Sun. It has monsterous storms and unbearably fast winds.

Neptune

▶ Neptune has the fastest winds of all the planets— they reach up to 930 mph (1,500km/h) close to its equator.

▶ Uranus is 1,736,000 mi. (2,800,000km) from the Sun. It is around four times the size of Earth and takes 84 years to make one orbit around the Sun.

Uranus

Jupiter

Saturn

◀ The gas giants are cold worlds. At the top of Saturn's clouds the temperature is as low as -220˚F (-140˚C). A layer of haze above the clouds gives the planet a smooth look.

◀ When we look at Jupiter, we see the top of its 620-mi. (1,000-km) -deep atmosphere. The white and red spots are raging storms. The wild storm called the Great Red Spot is clearly visible at the bottom.

Jupiter and Saturn

Jupiter is the largest giant. Earth would fit across its face 11 times, and it has a mass that is 2.5 times that of all the other planets combined. Young Jupiter was even bigger—five times its present size. The planet shrinks by around .8 in. (2cm) a year as it cools.

Saturn, the next largest, is almost twice as far from the Sun as Jupiter is. It is an imperfect ball shape—the region around its equator bulges. Saturn has very clear rings, and we get different views of these as the planet orbits the Sun. Sometimes we see them from above and at other times from below.

Stormy worlds

The top layers of Jupiter's and Saturn's gas atmospheres make colorful bands that go all the way around the planets. Storms grow and rage within the atmospheres of these two planets. A colossal storm on Jupiter, called the Great Red Spot, has been raging and swirling for more than 300 years. No one knows how much longer it could last, but it could potentially be seen for generations to come.

Moon families

Six planets have their own families of moons orbiting around them. The four gas giants have big families; Mars has two moons; and Earth has just one. The moons range in size from ball-shaped Ganymede, which is bigger than Mercury, down to village-sized, potato-shaped lumps such as Jupiter's Kale. The biggest are worlds in their own right and are as intriguing as any of the planets.

▲ The Italian astronomer Galileo Galilei (1564–1642) observed Jupiter's four largest moons—Io, Europa, Ganymede, and Callisto—with the newly invented telescope in 1610. They are now called the Galilean moons because he brought them to the attention of other astronomers and the public.

▼ Io travels above Jupiter's cloud tops. The image is deceiving: there are 217,000 mi. (350,000km)—roughly 2.5 Jupiters—between Io and Jupiter's clouds. Io, which is around the same size as Earth's Moon, circles Jupiter every 1.8 days.

Moon count

There are more than 140 moons orbiting the planets. We have known about Earth's Moon ever since the first humans saw it in our night sky; the others have only been discovered in the past 400 years. It is likely that all the big moons have been detected, but there are probably many more small ones still to be found.

Jupiter has the largest family of moons—it has at least 63. More than 40 of Jupiter's moons have been found since 2000, and more discoveries are expected.

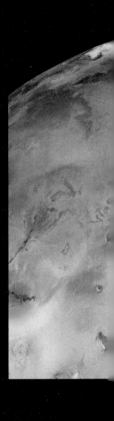

Origins

The moons of all the planets, aside from Earth, either formed as moons at the same time as their parent planet, or they started off as space rocks that were captured (pulled in toward the planet by its gravity) sometime in the past. For example, Jupiter's largest moons were made at the same time as the planet, but its smaller ones were originally space rocks. They traveled a little too close to Jupiter. As a result, its strong gravity pulled them into an orbit around the planet, where they now exist as moons.

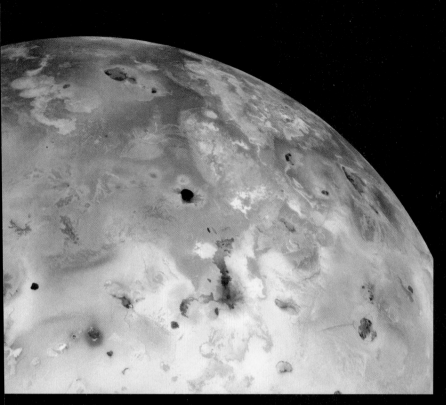

◄ Io is Jupiter's third-largest moon. It is a strange place, unlike anywhere else we know. Volcanoes are erupting on it all the time, and as a result, Io contains some of the hottest parts of the solar system. The dark green and black marks on the surface, shown here, are all volcanoes. When the volcanoes erupt, they can shoot hot gas and dust up to 186 mi. (300km) above the surface.

Contrasting worlds

More than 90 percent of the moons are less than 310 mi. (500km) across. The most recently discovered are the smallest of all at only 1 or 2 mi. (2 or 3km) wide. Those measuring less than around 198 mi. (320km) are irregular in shape, but they all look more or less the same—like lumps of barren rock!

The bigger moons are a regular ball shape. The largest is Jupiter's Ganymede, which has a diameter of 3,261 mi. (5,260km). The moons are made up of either rock, such as Ganymede, or a mix of rock and ice such as Neptune's Triton. Their surfaces are varied—they include cracks, grooves and craters, sulfur lakes, smooth ice plains, and ice volcanoes. Only one moon, Saturn's Titan, has a substantial atmosphere—it is completely covered in thick, orange clouds.

Oberon

Titania

Umbriel

URANUS

Miranda

Ariel

▲ Five of Uranus' 27 moons are shown here with the planet. Titania, the largest, is a little less than half the size of Earth's Moon. Oberon is a little smaller. Umbriel and Ariel are both around 719 mi. (1,160km) across. Cracks and cliffs can be seen on Ariel's surface, and grooves and a large mark can be seen on 291-mi. (470-km)-wide Miranda.

Dirty snowballs

Far beyond the planets, in the outer reaches of the solar system, are the comets. They are the most distant objects that orbit around the Sun. There are around ten trillion comets. They are mountain-sized dirty snowballs, usually too small and distant to be seen. Occasionally one travels close to Earth, and it can grow large enough and bright enough to be seen in the sky.

Cloud of comets

The comets make up the round Oort Cloud, which lies beyond the planetary part of the solar system. Its inside edge merges with the Edgeworth-Kuiper Belt (see page 35), and its outer edge is roughly 4,650 billion mi. (7,500 billion km) from us. Comets are a mix of around one-third rocky dust and two-thirds ice and snow. In 1951 the American astronomer Fred Whipple (1906–2004) described them as dirty snowballs, and that is what they have been nicknamed ever since. They have been like this since the solar system formed 4.6 billion years ago.

► Halley's Comet is named after Edmond Halley (1656–1742), who realized that the comets seen in 1531, 1607, and 1682 were all the same object. Here the comet is shown in Earth's sky in 1910, at a time when people still thought that seeing it brought bad luck.

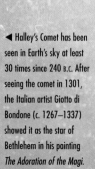

◄ Halley's Comet has been seen in Earth's sky at least 30 times since 240 B.C. After seeing the comet in 1301, the Italian artist Giotto di Bondone (c. 1267–1337) showed it as the star of Bethlehem in his painting *The Adoration of the Magi*.

▲ An area of trees measuring 12 sq. mi. (30km²) was uprooted in the Tunguska region of Siberia, Russia, in an explosion in June 1908. It is believed that the blast was caused by the breakup of a piece of comet, 3.7 mi. (6km) above the ground.

Traveling comets

Once in awhile a passing star knocks a comet out of the Oort Cloud and into the realm of the planets. Those that travel closer to the Sun than Mars change in a startling way. The Sun heats the comet and turns the snow on its surface into gas. This makes a gassy ball, called a coma, around the snowy nucleus (the dirty snowball part). The coma can grow up to 62,000 mi. (100,000km) across. As the comet heats up, gas and dust are pushed away from it and form tails, which are typically 62 million mi. (100 million km) long. Comets with large comas and long tails are big enough and bright enough to be seen from Earth. Around 800 have been seen so far, and at least ten more are sighted each year.

▶ The two tails of Comet Hale-Bopp were clearly visible when the comet was in Earth's sky in 1997. The gas tail is narrow and blue, while the broader, white dust tail is slightly curved.

Reaching Earth

When comets travel through the inner solar system, they shed large amounts of dust, which Earth can pass through as it orbits the Sun. Tiny bits of the dust, called meteoroids, heat up as they speed through Earth's atmosphere. As they burn, they produce short-lived streaks of light in the sky. These are known to us as meteors, or shooting stars. Thousands of them occur in Earth's atmosphere each year. A really bright meteor is called a fireball. Some meteoroids are rocks that are too big to burn up, and they crash onto Earth. These are meteorites.

SUMMARY OF CHAPTER 2: THE SUN & ITS FAMILY

Space neighbors

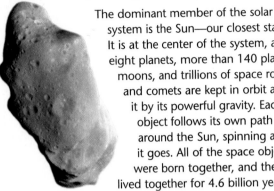

The dominant member of the solar system is the Sun—our closest star. It is at the center of the system, and eight planets, more than 140 planetary moons, and trillions of space rocks and comets are kept in orbit around it by its powerful gravity. Each object follows its own path around the Sun, spinning as it goes. All of the space objects were born together, and they have lived together for 4.6 billion years and will continue to do so far into the future.

The asteroid Ida

Solar system family

The four planets closest to the Sun—Mercury, Venus, Earth, and Mars—are balls of rock. Beyond them is the Main Belt of asteroids and then come the four biggest planets—Jupiter, Saturn, Uranus, and Neptune—that are all made of gas. The greater the distance from the Sun, the smaller it appears. The distant planets receive less of its heat and light.

While it was once known as the ninth planet, Pluto is now known as a dwarf planet. Pluto, this dark, icy world, is not a true planet because it is more like the space rocks of the Edgeworth-Kuiper Belt than like its closest planetary neighbors.

Covered in comets

Surrounding the planetary part of the solar system is an enormous, round shell of comets. These objects, described as dirty snowballs, are the most distant members of the solar system family. When one comes close to Earth, it gives us the chance to see an object in the sky that is normally far beyond our vision.

Growing family

There is still much to see and discover in the solar system. The number of objects that we know about goes up each year. Astronomers are sure that there are no new planets to discover, but they expect to find more moons circling the four biggest planets. The astronomers will discover more asteroids and Edgeworth-Kuiper Belt objects, and they will also learn more about the big solar system objects such as Jupiter's storms, Mars' rocks, and Earth's oceans.

Go further . . .

Discover planetary facts: www.dustbunny.com/afk/planets/

What is your weight on the Moon? www.exploratorium.edu/ronh/weight

Join a space club at: http://spaceplace.jpl.nasa.gov/en/kids/

Test your knowledge of the solar system at: http://starchild.gsfc.nasa.gov/docs/StarChild/StarChild.html

The Earth from the Air for Children by Yann Arthus-Bertrand (Thames & Hudson, Ltd., 2002)

There's No Place Like Space: All About Our Solar System by Tish Rabe (Random House, 1999)

Scientist
Someone who uses the rules and laws of nature to find out more about the world around us. An astronomer uses the rules of science to find out about the universe.

Planetary scientist
Studies the planets of the solar system and their moons.

Planetary geologist
Looks at the surface rocks and land formations on Mercury, Venus, Earth, Mars, and the Moon.

Cosmogonist
Examines the origin and general development of the solar system and other systems of stars with planets.

Visit Herschel's home and the museum located there: William Herschel Museum Bath, England BA12BL Phone: 44 01225 311 342 www.bath-preservation-trust.org.uk

Visit the Hall of Planet Earth and the Hall of the Meteorites at the American Museum of Natural History: Central Park West at 79th Street New York City, NY 10024-5192 Phone: (212) 769-5100 www.amnh.org

Spend an amazing day at a crater: Wolfe Creek meteorite crater Kununurra 6743, WA, Australia Phone: 61 08 9168 4200 www.calm.wa.gov.au/national_parks/previous_parks_month/wolfe_creek.html

Aerogel is an extraordinary substance—it is 99.8 percent air and is 1,000 times less dense than glass. It is being used on the *Stardust* mission to catch particles from a comet.

CHAPTER 3

Exploring the universe

We all like discovering things—about friends, where we live, or faraway places. When we want to discover more about something, we often try to get closer, to look for ourselves. Astronomers spend their lives finding out about the stars and planets. Unfortunately the stars and most of the solar system are too far away to be visited. Astronomers study the universe long-distance—relying on information coming across space to them. This is collected by Earth- and space-based telescopes. Robotic spacecraft are sent to explore solar system objects, and a dozen men have walked on the Moon. Future generations of space travelers will return to the Moon and travel to Mars to explore these worlds for themselves.

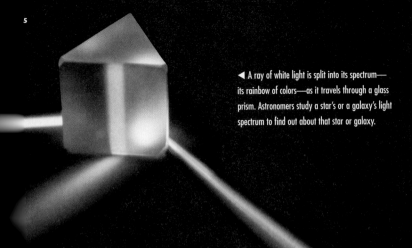

◄ A ray of white light is split into its spectrum—its rainbow of colors—as it travels through a glass prism. Astronomers study a star's or a galaxy's light spectrum to find out about that star or galaxy.

Space detective

A stronomers study the universe. They are interested in everything that is in it—from the planets, stars, and galaxies to how these parts fit together to make the whole. By learning about the universe today, they learn about its past and how it might develop in the future.

Looking out
Astronomers are based on Earth, but what they study is billions or trillions of miles away—too faraway for them to travel to. They work long-distance and let information come to them from across space.

Information from space
Stars and galaxies send out information in the form of energy, and one type of energy is light. By collecting this, our eyes make pictures and allow us to see things—our family, a book, or a galaxy. Other types of energy, such as radio, X-ray, infrared, and ultraviolet, are invisible to us. But astronomers' telescopes can collect and make pictures that we can see with these types of energy.

Starlight
All stars and galaxies have their own light—just as the Sun, our closest star, provides light. We see other objects, such as planets or moons, by starlight bouncing off their surfaces.

Looking into the distance
Light allows us to see objects in space. As we collect more light by using bigger telescopes, we can see more objects at a greater distance. We learn a lot by looking up at the sky with our eyes or a telescope, but close study of the light reveals even more information. Astronomers put a special instrument on the end of a telescope to split light into its spectrum—its rainbow of colors. By looking at this, they work out a star's temperature and what it is made of.

▲ If you had eyes that made pictures from infrared energy rather than light energy, this is what a pair of feet in sneakers would look like. Infrared is mostly heat energy. It is given off by anything with a temperature. In this image the hottest parts of the feet are colored red, warm parts are yellow, and cooler areas go through green and blue to mauve (coldest).

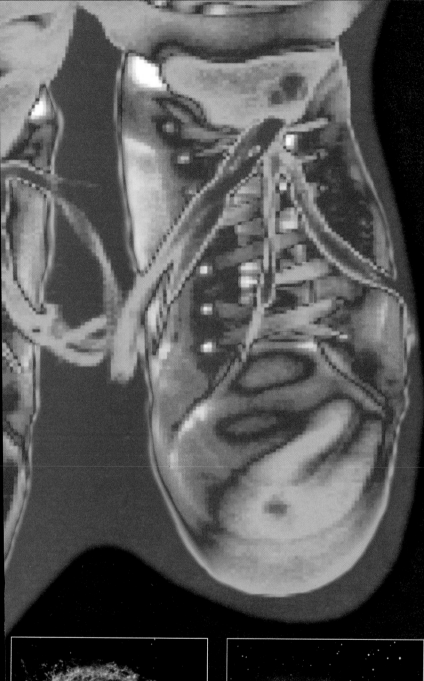

Complete picture

Light tells us a lot about an object, but not everything. Big chunks of some galaxies are invisible because we get no light from them, so we detect the region by its radio energy.

Elsewhere whole objects are only detected by energy other than light. Young, dim stars are invisible next to brighter stars, others are hidden by dust clouds. These stars are detected by their infrared energy.

A black hole gives off no light, but we know that it exists because of the X-ray energy around the hole.

Astronomers collect all the different types of energy to get as complete a picture as possible of the universe.

▼ Astronomers collect a range of energy from the galaxy M81. The images below show it in radio energy (top), infrared energy (bottom left), visible light (bottom center), and ultraviolet energy (bottom right). Each view shows different details of the galaxy's core of old stars and its spiral arms full of young, hot stars.

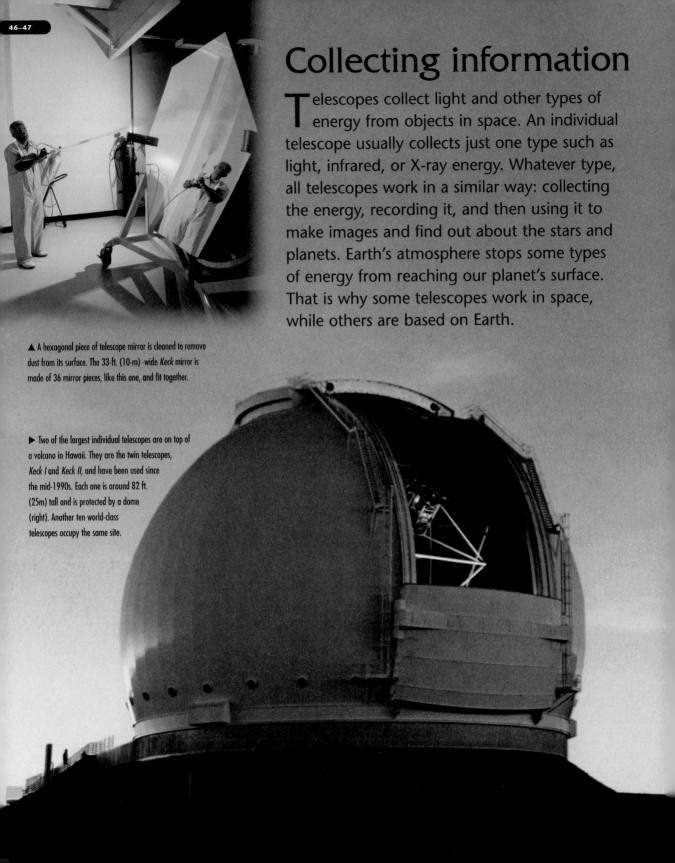

Collecting information

Telescopes collect light and other types of energy from objects in space. An individual telescope usually collects just one type such as light, infrared, or X-ray energy. Whatever type, all telescopes work in a similar way: collecting the energy, recording it, and then using it to make images and find out about the stars and planets. Earth's atmosphere stops some types of energy from reaching our planet's surface. That is why some telescopes work in space, while others are based on Earth.

▲ A hexagonal piece of telescope mirror is cleaned to remove dust from its surface. The 33-ft. (10-m) -wide *Keck* mirror is made of 36 mirror pieces, like this one, and fit together.

▶ Two of the largest individual telescopes are on top of a volcano in Hawaii. They are the twin telescopes, *Keck I* and *Keck II*, and have been used since the mid-1990s. Each one is around 82 ft. (25m) tall and is protected by a dome (right). Another ten world-class telescopes occupy the same site.

XMM-Newton Space Telescope

▼ These two telescopes, the European *XMM-Newton* and the American *Chandra*, have worked in space close to Earth. They have collected X-ray data about distant structures such as black holes and galaxies.

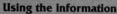

Chandra

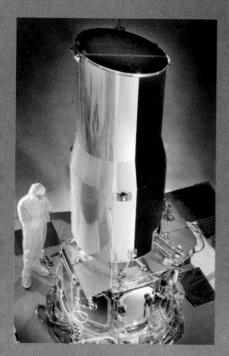

▲ Above, the *Spitzer Space Telescope* is being prepared for its launch in 2003. It collects infrared energy. The telescope has chilling systems to keep it cool. Without them, it would record its own heat energy instead of that of the planets, stars, and galaxies that it studies.

Telescopes in space

While astronomers have been using telescopes on Earth for almost 400 years (see page 38), they have only been looking at the universe through space-based telescopes for around 40 years. Space telescopes are used to collect the types of energy, such as X-ray energy, that cannot get through Earth's atmosphere. These minivan-sized telescopes orbit Earth looking out into space. They collect and record information 24 hours a day, all year-round, whatever the weather.

Using the information

Computers are very important to astronomers. They are used to work telescopes; they record and store information from space; and they help astronomers study the findings. No one needs to be close to a telescope to operate it, whether it is based on Earth or in space. Information is sent to a control room, and from there it is forwarded to the astronomer's own computer. These scientists live all over the world—many work in universities or for government organizations. They use the data from the stars and planets to help us understand and appreciate our universe.

Telescopes on Earth

The biggest and best light-collecting telescopes on Earth are on mountaintops. Light gets through Earth's atmosphere all the way down to sea level, but the mountaintop sites are above the clouds and away from city lights. The air is thin, dry, and still, allowing astronomers to get a great view of the universe. The telescopes are inside domes, and several can occupy the same location. An observatory is a site with more than one telescope.

Radio telescopes can also be found on Earth—they are usually on lower, flat ground, as radio waves can make it through Earth's atmosphere.

▼ You do not have to be an expert astronomer to enjoy the Moon, planets, and stars in the sky. You can see plenty with your eyes alone, and binoculars or a telescope will show you even more. It is a fascinating universe, so why not take a look at the sky at night?

Space robots

Robots have been exploring space for us for the past 40 years or so. They are not human-shaped robots but car-sized spacecraft consisting of a framework with tools attached. They are called space probes, and each one is designed to explore a specific target such as the Moon or Saturn. Some shoot past their targets, taking and recording information as they fly by. Some go into orbit around these distant worlds, and others land on them.

▲ *Genesis* completed its three-year mission in 2004. This involved traveling toward the Sun, collecting samples of its solar wind—atoms of the Sun in space—and returning these to Earth.

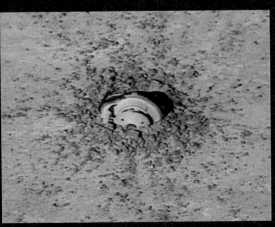

◀ The solar wind collected by *Genesis* was stored in a capsule. To try to make sure that this container survived the journey back to Earth, a clever retrieval plan was devised. As you can see in the test run pictured here, a parachute slowed down the capsule's fall. A long pole connected to a helicopter was then supposed to catch the container and carry it to the ground.

◀ Sadly the retrieval plan did not work, and *Genesis'* capsule crashed into the desert in Utah on September 8th, 2004. Its parachutes failed to open, and the container smashed into the ground at around 192 mph (310km/h). However, all was not lost— some of the solar wind atoms survived.

▲ It took seven years for *Cassini* to reach Saturn. On its arrival in July 2004 it went into orbit around the planet and started a four-year study of Saturn, its rings, and its moons. NASA extended this mission. *Cassini* celebrated ten years in space in June 2014.

Reaching the target

Space probes have started their journey by rocket or very occasionally by space shuttle. The United States has built the most probes. The Soviet countries sent many in the past, and now Japan and Europe explore space in this way.

Probes are sent to many types of solar system objects—they have been to all the planets and they have investigated the Sun, moons, comets, and asteroids.

Profile of a space probe

Space probes can look very different from each other and come in a range of sizes and shapes, depending on their goal. But they all have things in common. Each probe has a power source and a computer to control the mission and to deal with the data that it collects. A communication system sends and receives messages, and a set of tools and instruments is there in order to investigate the target.

Cassini at work

One of the largest and most complex space robots ever built, *Cassini* is the fourth space probe to investigate Saturn. American *Cassini* gave a ride to *Huygens*, a smaller European probe, which is designed to descend by parachute through the murky atmosphere of Titan and down to its surface. Between them they carry 18 instruments, tools, and cameras to find and record data.

▼ Aerogel (see page 43) is onboard the *Stardust* space probe—the first-ever mission to collect comet particles. It is a spongelike solid that is made up of 99.8 percent air. It is an excellent insulator against heat—that is why the crayons, which are lying on the aerogel in the picture, are not melting in spite of being heated.

Landers & rovers

Space robots have landed on the Moon, Venus, Mars, and the asteroid Eros. Once on the surface, the space probes—called landers—turn on, look around, and then investigate. Some move around, others stay still. The landers work while they have power—this can be for months. When their job is done, they stay forever on their new home.

Getting there

One of the most difficult parts of a lander's mission is arriving safely. It needs to slow down after its supersonic journey from Earth. The aim is a soft, controlled landing, rather than a crash. This is done by using small rockets, parachutes, if there is an atmosphere, or blow-up balls to cushion the lander's fall and bounce it to a halt. Scientists on Earth are in contact as the lander comes down. Its landing site is always carefully chosen, but the exact location of the touchdown is unknown until the lander has stopped.

▲ This computer chip is onboard the Mars rover *Opportunity*. It has around 35,000 laser-engraved signatures on it. These are from people who visited *Spirit* and *Opportunity* as they were built.

▶ The camera high up on *Spirit*, the Mars rover, surveys the landscape, looking for interesting rock or soil sites for the craft to move to. The "rat" (rock abrasion tool) on the tool arm (near the front wheels) scrapes away the top layers of a rock to see underneath it.

▲ Seven *Surveyor* landers were sent to the Moon between 1966 and 1968. Two crash-landed. The other five, including *Surveyor 3* (above), landed safely, took pictures, and tested the surface for the astronauts who would follow. *Apollo 12* landed (on horizon) close to *Surveyor 3* in November 1969.

Standing still

Some landers investigate just their place of landing—they do not move around. The most successful lander missions were some of the *Surveyor* probes on the Moon in the 1960s and the two *Viking* landers on Mars in 1976.

Others missions have landed on Venus and on Eros. Between 1970 and 1982 eight *Venera* crafts survived the journey through its thick atmosphere to land on Venus. In 2001 *NEAR* studied Eros from above its surface. Once this job was done, the craft landed on the asteroid—an added bonus to its mission.

Roving around

Landers that move around are nicknamed "rovers." Five rovers have been sent into space. Two *Lunokhod* crafts worked on the Moon in the 1970s. *Sojourner* traveled across Mars in 1997, and in 2004 *Opportunity* and *Spirit* did the same. These twin rovers used a camera and tools to study rocks and soil and to look for past signs of liquid water on Mars.

1. *Tumbleweed*, a new rover, is currently being tested for use on planets and moons. It is an inflated ball containing instruments. Here, the windblown rover is bouncing along.

2. *Tumbleweed* comes to a stop at an area of scientific interest on the planet that it is investigating. Once it has reached a standstill, the rover deflates.

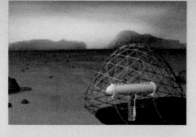

3. Now you can see a cutaway diagram of the rover. At this stage instruments and a drill are used to take measurements and samples from the surface.

4. *Tumbleweed* transmits information to an orbiting satellite that sends the data back to Earth. Once it has finished, the rover reinflates itself and sets off again on its journey.

Life search

There are billions of living things in the universe. Humans are just one type; many more creatures and plants live on land and in the water. Some are single-celled structures, others are multi-billion-celled intelligent beings. All have one thing in common—they live on planet Earth. As far as we know, there is no life outside Earth. Most astronomers believe that it is there, and some are searching for it. But for now, its form and home remain a mystery.

◄ Some astronomers once thought intelligent creatures lived on Mars. This 1936 comic strip shows how one artist imagined extraterrestrial life. Today's cartoons continue to fantasize about strange-looking aliens.

► Life is found in unexpected places on Earth, and it survives in extreme conditions. This sea anemone is living 2.2 mi. (3.5km) below the surface, where there is no light.

▼ Life on Earth became land-based around 400 million years ago. Humans—the dominant form of life on Earth—have been here for around two million years.

Life on Earth

There has been life on Earth for around 3.8 billion years—that is more than three fourths of the planet's lifetime. It started with single-celled ocean life. This evolved into complex plants and animals in Earth's oceans and on its land. Today life is found in all types of places. By studying it, we have learned what life outside Earth needs in order to begin and to survive and where it might be. We are looking in places that have liquid water, carbon (the most common atom in living things), other elements, such as nitrogen, and energy such as sunlight or lightning.

Life elsewhere in the solar system

Mars is not suitable for life today, but it may have been the home of primitive life in the past. Its water is frozen now, but around 3.5 billion years ago it was liquid. Perhaps life developed in Mars' water as it did in Earth's.

In 1976 two space probes tested Mars' surface for indications of life; none were found. Future probes to Europa and Mars may find signs of life. Saturn's moon, Titan, was once thought inhospitable, but the discovery of life in harsh conditions on Earth means that this moon is another place where life might exist.

▼ This computer-generated image shows what Mars might have looked like 3.5 billion years ago. A river of water cuts through the rocky landscape, and the Sun shines in the Martian sky.

▲ *Darwin* is a group of eight spacecraft. Six of the spacecraft are space telescopes, and the seventh combines the light collected by all of the telescopes. The eighth will communicate with Earth and the rest of the group. Together they will scan the nearby universe for worlds like Earth and then look for gases that could indicate signs of life.

Beyond the solar system

Astronomers are searching for primitive life in the solar system— anything sophisticated would have been found by now. But the search beyond is very different.

Our galaxy has thousands of planets and moons that are capable of harboring life. Perhaps one is like Earth and home to someone like you. Finding out is not easy—the closest star with planets is beyond our reach. A space probe would take billions of years to get there. But intelligent life makes noise. We have been listening for noise signals for around 40 years but have heard nothing—yet.

Journey of a lifetime

A trip into space is one of the most exciting and memorable things that a human being can do. Around 400 men and women have made the trip, and there are plenty more who are eager to follow. Almost all of the astronauts have gone into space immediately around Earth. Only 26 have ventured farther—to our Moon. In the decades ahead we will go even farther. For now, we are just discovering what it is like to live and work away from our familiar home on Earth.

▲ Astronauts onboard the International Space Station (ISS) have to cope without the help of gravity—even simply moving around is a challenge. The weightless conditions affect the human body: in this picture André Kuipers wears equipment that records changes in his body as he moves around.

Space and the human body

The human body is designed to live on Earth—we breathe oxygen, live in warm temperatures, and are used to the pull of gravity. It is different a few hundred miles above our planet where astronauts live and work. There, where they do not feel gravity's pull, they are weightless and float around. The temperature is either high enough to toast them or low enough to freeze them, and there is no oxygen. They are safe inside their spacecraft but need the protection of space suits once they are outside.

Most astronauts feel sick at the beginning of a trip. This does not last, but some discomfort lingers. In the weightless environment body fluids are not pulled downward by gravity, and this can feel strange. The heart does not have to pump as hard to get blood around the body, the nose gets blocked, and the face gets puffy. The important thing is to eat well and exercise in order to stay fit and healthy.

Men on the Moon
Of the 26 American men who traveled to the Moon in six missions between 1969 and 1972, 12 walked on its surface, and all returned home. The 12 took photographs, collected 857 lbs. (388kg) of rock and soil, and set up experiments. No one has been back since, but there are plans to return.

▼ The *Lunar Roving Vehicle* was used on three Moon missions. American Eugene Cernan, seen here, was the commander of *Apollo 17*, the final mission. He was the last man to walk on the Moon.

◄ The ISS is being built and used by 16 countries. It has grown bit by bit since the first piece arrived in space by rocket in 1998. Later pieces, crew, and supplies have been ferried to the ISS by space shuttles and rockets. Crew have lived onboard since 2000.

Target Mars
Mars is the next new place humans will visit. We are not going there yet though—we need a new vehicle for the journey, and we are still learning about the planet. A trip to Mars and back would last around three years, so we need to know that a crew could cope over such a long time.

For the time being astronauts are staying closer to Earth—onboard the ISS, which orbits our planet. All that they learn there about life in space will help put them one step closer to Mars.

▼ A space suit provides oxygen for breathing and keeps an astronaut's temperature at a safe level. American Rex Walheim wears his as he works outside the ISS in April 2002.

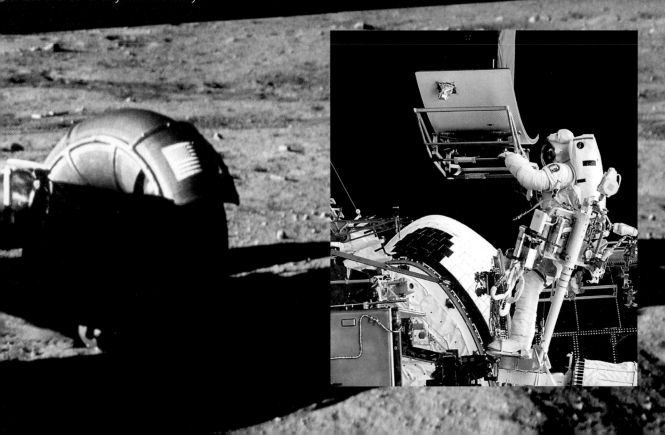

◀ Before this century is over, you may become a space tourist, staying in a vacation city orbiting around Earth. What you would find there is a series of linked hotels and leisure areas. You would spend the night in a bolted down sleeping bag to stop you from floating around. During the day you could leap around in the gymnastics hall or simply admire the view from an observation gallery, where artificial gravity would help you stay still.

The future

Astronomers know a lot about the universe, but they realize that there is still a lot to learn. They would like to answer questions about worlds local to Earth, such as what is Pluto really like, and was there ever life on Mars? They would also like to know more about the distant galaxies and stars. A new breed of telescopes and spacecraft will help the astronomers make new discoveries and answer their questions. In the far future humans living on the Moon or Mars will uncover new information themselves.

▲ At the moment we can send only rovers to Mars. But it is possible that within 50 years astronauts will travel to this planet.

Space probes of the future

Astronomers and space scientists are constantly planning future missions and new space probes. Pluto, Mars, and Jupiter's moon, Europa, are already in their sights. A future goal is to bring back pieces of planets and moons to Earth to study them.

The stars are too far away for a space probe mission right now. But engineers are working on ideas for faster spacecraft. In the distant future we may reach out of our solar system.

Humans in space

New vehicles to take humans to Mars and the Moon are being designed. Today's astronauts will be too old to carry out the work planned. They are relying on future generations to carry on where they left off. Will yours be the first human footprint on Mars?

Telescopes of the future

Bigger and better telescopes will help astronomers see more of the universe in the decades ahead. The bigger a telescope is, the more and farther astronomers can see. Ones that have large, single mirrors that sag are unusable. Future mirrors will be made of many smaller pieces, allowing huge telescopes to be built. Astronomers will also link telescopes across Earth. These will be able to work together to show us more of the universe.

▶ The *James Webb Space Telescope* is being prepared to take over from the *Hubble Space Telescope*, which is in space now. It will work for about ten years and then be replaced by another telescope.

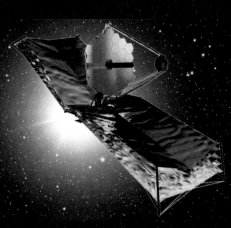

SUMMARY OF CHAPTER 3: EXPLORING THE UNIVERSE

Curiosity

Humans have always been curious about where they live. Not just about Earth but also about what lies farther away in our solar system and beyond. People have been learning about the universe for thousands of years. At first they just used their eyes. Then around 400 years ago they turned the newly invented telescope upward. It soon revealed unimagined wonders: worlds never seen before such as Jupiter's moons and stars galore.

The *Genesis* space probe collected samples of particles of solar wind.

Tools of exploration

The telescope has been the astronomer's basic tool since it was first used. Today's telescopes are enormous—they see much farther and in more detail, but like the first, they collect light from the stars and planets and form it into pictures. Telescopes are now based on Earth and in space, and they also collect other types of energy such as radio, X-ray, or infrared. All types of information are used to give us a better understanding of the universe.

Robotic craft

Space probes regularly explore solar system objects for us. They make discoveries and show us new and familiar objects close-up. Without them we would not know what the planet Neptune or a comet's nucleus look like, nor understand what it is like on the surface of Mars.

The astronomer

Telescopes and space probes are important because they collect information from space. But a third tool—the astronomer's brain—is essential. The astronomer analyzes the information to find out more about the universe. When results have been examined and conclusions drawn from data that we have available, the astronomer decides what new questions we would like to answer and how we will do this in the future.

Go further . . .

Read about the ISS: www.spaceflight.nasa.gov/station

Download models of spacecraft to build: www.jpl.nasa.gov/scalemodels

Want to be an astronaut?: www.esa.int/esaHS/ ESA1RMGBCLC_astronauts_0.html

Try out some training exercises at: www.edspace.nasa.gov/text/astroschool

Space Exploration by Carole Stott, (Dorling Kindersley, 2004)

Stargazing: Astronomy without a Telescope by Patrick Moore (CUP, 2000)

Space scientist
Works with spacecraft.

Astronaut
Man or woman who travels to space.

Telescope operator
Operates Earth-based or space-based telescopes on behalf of astronomers.

Astrobiologist
Someone who studies the origin and evolution of life.

Radio astronomer
Collects radio data from space and uses it to learn about the universe.

Astrophotographer
Takes photographs of the night sky and of individual objects in it.

Visit the Kennedy Space Center, where you can walk around spacecraft and question an astronaut:
Kennedy Space Center
Cape Canaveral, FL
Phone: (321) 449-4444
www.kennedyspacecenter.com

Get up close to spacecraft at:
Cité de L'Espace space park:
Toulouse, France 31506
Phone: 33 05 62 71 56 05
www.cite-espace.com

Learn more about living in space at:
The Science Museum
London, England SW7 2DD
Phone: 44 0870 870 4868
www.sciencemuseum.org.uk

Glossary

absolute magnitude
A measure of the true brightness of a star.

amateur
Someone who does something as a hobby. An amateur astronomer is someone who studies the stars and planets in their free time.

apparent magnitude
A measure of the brightness of a star seen from Earth.

asteroid
A space rock orbiting the Sun. Most asteroids are in the Main Belt.

astronaut
A person who travels into space.

astronomer
A person who studies the universe and everything in it beyond Earth.

astronomy
The study of everything in space—all space objects and space itself.

atmosphere
Gases held around a planet or moon by its gravity. A star's atmosphere is the gas held beyond its photosphere.

atom
The smallest part of an element.

big bang
The explosion that scientists believe created our universe, space, and time around 13 billion years ago.

billion
One thousand million (one followed by nine zeros).

brightness
A measure of a star's light.

cluster
A group of galaxies or stars held together by gravity.

comet
A small snow, ice, and dust object, nicknamed a dirty snowball.

constellation
A piece of sky where bright stars form an imaginary pattern such as that of a human or an animal.

crater
A bowl-shaped hollow on the surface of a planet, moon, or asteroid formed by a space rock crashing into it.

dark matter
The material in the universe that it is not possible to find; it makes up as much as 95 percent of the universe.

Edgeworth-Kuiper Belt
The flat belt of icy space rocks beyond the orbit of Neptune.

element
A basic substance of nature such as hydrogen, oxygen, and carbon.

ellipse
A two-dimensional shape; a long circle.

equator
An imaginary line drawn around the middle of a planet, moon, or star. It divides the top (northern) half from the bottom (southern) half.

fireball
A very bright meteor.

flyby
A space probe that journeys to a planet or moon and then records information as it flies past its target. "Flyby" is also used to describe this type of mission.

galactic black hole
A massive, dense hole in space at the center of a galaxy.

galaxy
A vast collection of stars, gas, and dust that are held together by gravity.

gas giants
The four largest planets, which are mostly made up of gas—Jupiter, Saturn, Uranus, and Neptune.

globular cluster
A ball-shaped group of old stars that exist together.

gravity
A force of attraction. The Sun's gravity pulls on Earth, and Earth's gravity pulls on you.

hexagonal
A six-sided shape.

lava
Molten (hot, liquid) rock that flows out of a planet or moon (*see* volcano).

light-year
A unit used to measure distances across the universe. One light-year is the distance light travels in one year.

magnetic field
Region of space around a planet or star where the magnetism produced by the planet or star is felt.

Main Belt
The doughnut-shaped belt of asteroids between Mars and Jupiter.

maria (singular: mare)
Dark markings on the Moon—large depressions in the surface that were flooded by volcanic lava in the past.

mass
The amount of material in an object. A star of eight solar masses has eight times the amount of material as the Sun.

meteor
The streak of light produced by a meteoroid as it travels through Earth's atmosphere.

meteorite
A space rock that lands on Earth, another planet, or a moon.

meteoroid
A tiny piece of dust from a comet or asteroid.

Milky Way
The galaxy we live in. Also the name of the path of stars seen in Earth's sky.

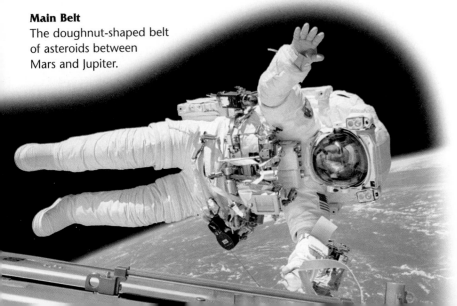

million
One thousand thousand (one followed by six zeros).

moon
A rock, or rock and ice body, that orbits around a planet or an asteroid.

nebula
A cloud of gas and dust in space.

neutron star
A small, densely-packed star produced in a supernova explosion.

nuclear reaction
The process that takes place inside a star when elements are changed to other elements.

observatory
A building or group of buildings that house telescopes.

Oort Cloud
The huge shell of comets around the planetary part of the solar system.

opaque
Foggy; not allowing light to pass through; not see-through.

open cluster
A group of young, bright stars, which will eventually drift apart.

orbit
The path one object takes around another, more massive object. The Moon orbits Earth, and Earth orbits the Sun.

photosphere
Visible layer of a star, e.g. the Sun.

planet
A large, round body made up of rock or gas that orbits a star.

planetary nebula
A type of star. It consists of an expanding, colorful cloud of gas and dust, which has been ejected by the dying star at the center of the cloud.

professional
Someone who does something as their job. A professional astronomer is paid to study the stars and planets.

protostar
A very young star.

pulsar
A neutron star that is identified by its beams of energy. The energy pulses across space as the star spins.

ring system
A collection of rings around a planet.

rock planets
The four planets closest to the Sun—Mercury, Venus, Earth, and Mars. Also called the inner planets.

satellite
An object that is held in orbit around a planet or moon by gravity. A telescope in orbit around Earth is a man-made satellite. The Moon is a natural satellite of Earth.

solar eclipse
The effect achieved when the Moon is between the Sun and Earth and the Moon's shadow falls on Earth.

Solar Nebula
The spinning cloud of gas and dust that formed into the solar system.

solar system
The Sun and all the objects that orbit it: eight planets, more than 140 moons, space rocks, and comets.

solar wind
A stream of the particles blown away from the Sun that make up the Sun's atoms.

space probe
A type of spacecraft, also called a probe. An unmanned, robotic craft sent to look at solar system objects.

space rock
A small rock or icy rock object that orbits the Sun.

spectrum
The rainbow band of colors produced when light is split.

star
A ball of hot, bright gas that produces energy by nuclear reaction.

stellar
Of or relating to a star.

stellar black hole
The remains of a star that has collapsed in on itself.

sunspot
A dark, cool patch on the surface of the Sun.

supercluster
A number of clusters of galaxies held together by gravity.

supernova
A massive star that has suddenly exploded and shines brightly.

supernova remnant
The gas and dust remains of a supernova explosion.

telescope
An instrument that uses lenses, mirrors, or a combination of the two to collect light from a distant object and form that light into an image. Telescopes also collect radio, X-ray, infrared, and ultraviolet energy.

trillion
One million million (one followed by 12 zeros).

universe
Everything that exists—all of space and everything in it.

volcano
Mountains made out of material that started off inside a planet. Molten rock (lava) bursts through the planet's crust and flows onto its surface, building a volcano in the process.

Index

Acknowledgments

The publisher would like to thank the following for permission to reproduce their material. Every care has been taken to trace copyright holders. However, if there have been unintentional omissions or failure to trace copyright holders, we apologize and will, if informed, endeavor to make corrections in any future edition.

Key: *b* = bottom, *c* = center, *l* = left, *r* = right, *t* = top

pages: front cover (*left to right*) NASA/Hubble Space Telescope, NASA/JPL, Science Photo Library/NASA; 1 Science Photo Library/Jerry Lodriguss (SPL); 2 SPL/NASA; 4–5 NASA; 7*t* SOHO/NASA; 8*bl* Corbis/Bill Varie; 8–9*t* NASA/ESA/S.Beckwith(STScI)/HUDF Team; 9*cl* SPL/Royal Observatory, Edinburgh; 9*cr* NASA/JPL; 9*bl* STScI/AURA; 9*br* SPL/NOAO; 10*bl* Corbis/Bettmann; 10*tr* Galaxy Picture Library/Robin Scagell 11*tl* Galaxy /Robin Scagell; 11*tc* SPL/Celestial Image; 11*tr* SPl/NASA/Space Telescope Science Institute; 13*br* Corbis/David Zimmerman; 14*l* Corbis/ Bettmann; 15*tr* National Gallery, London; 15*br* SPL/Eckhard Slawik; 16*tr* Getty Imagebank; 17*tl* Galaxy/Robin Scagell; 17*cr* Alamy/Photo Network; 18*l* NASA; 18–19 Bridgeman Art Library/ Villa Farnesina, Rome; 19*tr* SPL/ Pekka Parviainen; 19*bl* NASA/JPL; 20*l* Galaxy/Swedish Solar Vacuum Telescope; 20–21*bc* SPL/NASA/ Space Telescope Institute; 21*tc* and *tr* David Malin Images/Anglo-Australian Observatory; 22*bl* SPL/David Hardy; 22–23*t* SPL/NASA; 23*tr* SPL/Russell Kightley; 23*br* Corbis; 24–25 NASA/Stefan Seip; 24*br* SOHO/NASA; 25*cl* Galaxy Swedish Solar Vacuum Telescope; 25*bc* Bridgeman Art Library/Private Collection; 25*br* Corbis/Galen Rowell; 27 SPL/NASA; 28*bl* Corbis/Bettmann; 29*br* Galaxy/Calvin J. Hamilton; 30*cl* Corbis/Brian Vikander; 30–31*b* Alamy/Goodshoot; 31*tc* Corbis/Peter Turnley; 31*c* Getty Imagebank; 31*cr* Corbis/Jonathan Blair; 32*tl* Corbis/Araldo de Luca; 32*bl* NASA/JPL; 32–33 SPL/NASA/SMU/David P. Anderson; 33*tr* NASA; 34*cl* Galaxy/Gareth Williams; 34*c* Galaxy/NASA; 34*cr* Galaxy/NASA; 35*tl* Galaxy/NASA; 35*tr* Corbis/Bettmann; 35*br* NASA/JPL; 36*tl* Art Archive/Palazzo de Te Mantua/Dagli Orti; 36*br* Corbis/Araldo de Luca; 38*tl* Corbis; 38*bl* NASA/JPL; 39*tl* NASA/Steve Lee, Jim Bell, Mike Wolff; 39*b* SPL/NASA; 40*bl* Art Archive/Scrovegni Chapel, Padua/Dagli Orti; 40*tr* Corbis/Bettmann; 40*br* Novosti News Agency, London; 41 Galaxy/Robin Scagell; 42*tl* Galaxy/NASA; 43 NASA/JPL; 44*tl* SPL/David Parker; 44–45 SPL/Sir Arthur Tucker; 45*bc* and *bl* NASA/JPL; 45*cr* and *br* NASA/UIT; 46*tl*, and 46–47 Corbis/Roger Ressmeyer; 47*tl* NASA/SCOPE; 47*tc* European Space Agency (ESA); 47*tr* ESA/NASA; 47*bc* Corbis/Gabe Palmer; 48*tl* NASA/JPL; 48*cl* SPL/NASA; 48*bl* SPL/NASA; 48–49 ESA; 49*br* NASA/JPL; 50*bl* SPL/NASA; 50*tr* NASA/JPL; 50–51 NASA/JPL; 51*tr* NASA/JPL (x4); 52*tl* Art Archive/Eileen Tweedy; 52*bl* Corbis/Bill Ross; 52*cr* SPL/B. Murton; 53*tl* ESA; 53*tr* SPL/ESA; 53*b* SPL/Kees Veenenbos; 54*tl* ESA; 54–55 SPL/NASA; 55*tc* NASA; 55*br* NASA; 56–57 SPL/Victor Habbick; 57*tr* NASA; 57*br* NASA; 58*tl* NASA/JPL; 59*br* NAA/JPL; 60*bl* SPL/NASA; 61*tr* NSF/AURA/NOAO; 64*bl* Alamy/Imagestate

The publisher would like to thank the following illustrators:
Julian Baum (14–15, 29, 37), Mark Bristow (28–29),
Sebastian Quigley (10–11, 12–13, 16–17)